STRAIGHT'S SUITE
FOR CRAIG COTTER & FRANK O'HARA

STRAIGHT'S SUITE
FOR CRAIG COTTER & FRANK O'HARA

WILLIAM HEYEN

MAYAPPLE PRESS 2012

Published by   MAYAPPLE PRESS
                362 Chestnut Hill Rd.
                Woodstock, NY 12498
                www.mayapplepress.com

ISBN 978-1-936419-11-1

Cover art, "View over Mecox" by Jane Freilicher, courtesy Tibor de Nagy Gallery, New York, and courtesy of the Memorial Art Gallery of the University of Rochester, gift of Lynne Lovejoy in memory of her husband Dr. Frank Lovejoy, Jr.

Cover designed by Judith Kerman. Book designed and typeset by Amee Schmidt with titles in ITC Avant Garde Gothic and text in Californian FB.

Also by William Heyen

POETRY

Depth of Field (1970, re-issued 2005)
Noise in the Trees: Poems and a Memoir (1974)
The Swastika Poems (1977)
Long Island Light: Poems and a Memoir (1979)
The City Parables (1980)
Lord Dragonfly: Five Sequences (1981, re-issued 2010)
Erika: Poems of the Holocaust (1984)
The Chestnut Rain (1986)
Brockport, New York: Beginning with "And" (1988)
Pterodactyl Rose: Poems of Ecology (1991)
Ribbons: The Gulf War (1991)
The Host: Selected Poems 1965-1990 (1994)
Crazy Horse in Stillness (1996)
Diana, Charles, & the Queen (1998)
Shoah Train (2003)
The Rope (2003)
The Confessions of Doc Williams & Other Poems (2006)
To William Merwin: A Poem (2007)
A Poetics of Hiroshima (2008)
The Angel Voices: A Poem (2010)
The Football Corporations (2012)

PROSE

Vic Holyfield & the Class of 1957: A Romance (1986)
With Me Far Away: A Memoir (1994)
Pig Notes & Dumb Music: Prose on Poetry (1998)
The Hummingbird Corporation (2003)
Home: Autobiographies, Etc. (2004)
The Cabin: Journal 1964-1984 (2012)

ANTHOLOGIES

A Profile of Theodore Roethke (Ed. 1971)
American Poets in 1976 (Ed. 1976)
The Generation of 2000: Contemporary American Poets (Ed. 1984)
Dumb Beautiful Ministers: Poets from the Long Island Quarterly (Ed. 1996)
September 11, 2001: American Writers Respond (Ed. 2002)

GALLERY

1.	(Brockport Power)	7
2.	(Vision)	8
3.	(American Poetry)	9
4.	(Film)	10
5.	(Request)	11
6.	(Montauk)	12
7.	(Rose)	13
8.	(Circuit)	14
9.	(Portraits)	16
10.	(The Strand)	18
11.	(Roethke)	19
12.	(Art)	20
13.	(Meat / Flesh)	21
14.	(The Modern)	24
15.	(Winter Urine)	25
16.	(Inquiry)	26
17.	("*Simplicity! Simplicity! Simplicity!*")	27
18.	(Still, Life)	28
19.	(Eclipse: Dear Craig & Frank,)	29
20.	(Compensation)	31
21.	(Postscript)	32
22.	(Ardor)	33
23.	(The Stranger)	34
24.	(Fellow Feeling)	35
25.	(Tony Bennett)	37
26.	(Changes of Administration)	38
27.	(Desert)	44
28.	(Toupee Song)	45
29.	(Song)	46
30.	(The Happening)	47
31.	(Projection)	48
32.	(Closet Hangover *Pillow Talk* Syntax)	49
33.	(Survivors)	50
34.	(New Lives)	51
35.	(The Circular Units)	52
36.	(Queen)	56
37.	(A Flower)	57
38.	(Night Scene)	58
39.	(Dream Track)	60
40.	(Train)	61
41.	(Seventeen)	63
42.	(The New York School)	64

43. (Peonies)   65
44. (3/12/11)   67
45. (Simulated)   68
46. (A Question of Color)   69
47. (Listening to the Sun)   70
48. (Pitch)   72
49. (Coherence)   73
50. (Email from Cotter on O'Hara's Birthday)   77
51. (The Roses, 2011)   79
52. (Country Mouse)   80

Preface

A suite, amen, a succession of lyric paintings—no table of contents here but a "gallery"—in related keys & tones, each seeming to evoke the next until, as a whole, this *Straight's Suite* serves to answer a question addressed to Frank O'Hara's ghost: "What's the theory of art where you are?" The poet-speaker, from his first breaths, thinking of the iconic O'Hara at work at the Museum of Modern Art, declares himself resident at his own reception desk "& ready to receive." He wants to understand "intuitive gay ways [he's] just begun to fathom," yearns for a capacious democratic structure of thought & fellow-feeling within & without.

What he immediately receives is a memory of himself as a boy of nine who witnesses a primal sexual scene & who then dives "into brine / into the season of jellyfish," their "filaments trailing into the blue-green" as these spermatozoic creatures blip against his mask. Poets stake claim to certain words. These filaments, and later in this book Heyen's oscillations, arrive from Walt Whitman. In homage to America's greatest poem, "Song of Myself," *Straight's Suite* is 52 lyrics long. And these arrive to the poet largely by way of what I've described elsewhere as "a staring with memory & the auditory mind." There is no other invocation in contemporary poetry as plaintive as Heyen's when he prays to O'Hara, "Angel, bundle with Walt across my portal."

Oscillations: affections & suspicions; tight forms & the trying-out of loose & perhaps non-consequential O'Hara probes; ardor & sadness; the personal & the distanced; elegance & squalor; dream & the quotidien (Arab Spring & Fukushima); sometimes, a desire for the high seriousness that seems for Heyen lacking in the O'Hara / New York School / Beat / Projectivist aesthetics, & the realization of a concurrent need: "we'll resuscitate & bandage & mourn & rebuild & bury / as best we can, but let's / once more, for old time's sake, party." Art need not always tend toward tragic or comic or romantic closure.

What are the connections between any individual's sexuality & his/her aesthetic? Well, in any case, Heyen asks O'Hara how "I might get my poem to *be* its subject, / not just be about it." He realizes that this has always been everything for art to ask for.

Edwina Seaver
London / 2012

1.   (Brockport Power)

I've been to MoMA only once. I didn't know, then,
Frank, you'd worked there. At your reception desk
I hoped for reciprocal perks
with my own gallery in Rochester. No luck,

I paid full fare . . . but Lucian Freud jolted me awake
that one hour I had before my talk
on Lucien Stryk at AWP, meeting
at the Broadway Sheraton—his life in Zen that . . .

hey, the power's back on, right in mid-sentence,
that orgasm'd out at breakfast (my usual granola
laced with juice). Even my down-
stairs gas stove's pilot needs electric

but I could blue a burner with my butane lighter,
so had my mug of instant meditation. . . .
My wife's asleep upstairs. I'm retired, free
at my own reception desk, & ready to receive.

2.   (Vision)

A Town of Smithtown beach on the Sound
called Little Africa. I was maybe nine.
Fake parrots in scrub oaks, monkey howls.
I peed at a urinal, then climbed a divider

to look over a shower where
I knew the high school guys were.
Their trunks were at their feet,
they all had hard-ons,

& were jerking off, laughing. Maybe a contest—
who had the biggest, who could shoot first.
I got down & ran out into sunshine,
pulled on flippers & snorkel,

took dizzying breaths & dove into brine
into the season of jellyfish, thousands of spawn
drifting in against the beach, blipping my mask,
filaments trailing into the blue-green.

3.   (American Poetry)

Frank, you've got me wondering how
I might get my poem to *be* its subject,
not just be about it, if it ain't now.
I keep hearing a frog going *ribet, ribet,*

all night, not exactly singing but,
yes, communing with its fellows. See it
where a snapper is about to interrupt it.
Eight lines, a green meal, no frog esthetic.

4.   (FILM)

That poem of yours to the film industry—
such sincere camp
Joe LeSeuer says somebody like John Hollander
is pretty good in his own movie poem but

"possessed of a sensibility
too determinedly heterosexual" so couldn't
pull off what you do how
you evoke "Crossing Brooklyn Ferry"

whose voice addresses the hidden world—
"You necessary film continue to envelop the soul"—
as you now stare into the star system in the clouds
& dispense your assent which is like a prayer,

amen, yes, you really hit it this time Frank amen—
"Roll on, reels of celluloid, as the great earth rolls on!"—
& maybe this is what Edward G. Robinson is thinking
while filming *Soylent Green* his last flick as he

checks himself in for death to be administered
& insists on the full fifteen minutes or was it twenty
of nature footage while sedatives & poisons work in him
deer in golden fields the thrilling waves of birds

his cop friend Thorne can't save him now
nothing will save us now from death & beauty
as we eat our bodies crossing Brooklyn by ferry
"Roll on, reels of celluloid, as the Great earth rolls on!"

5.   (Request)

Frank, I haven't met him in person
but poet Craig Cotter in California
sent me his books & it's touching
how much he loves you though

he never met you. Why don't you assume form
from your Green River Cemetery
to engage with him, do me the favor, won't you,
while I walk the grounds this spring?

Cotter will be mesmerized
from time with you that would always be,
as Joe LeSeuer says, transformed, & holding
special promise, an alchemy

you brought about so effortlessly
by way of riveting energy whose source,
Joe says, "must have been
a fearless love of life."

I want to leave you alone with Craig.
While you're enfolding him, I'll be reading you
to hold you in this dimension. Would you
do this for me? Can you?

6.   (MONTAUK)

Joe says you hit lots of short poems perfect
with one draft. Well, I haven't spotted any,
but never mind me. But does it really matter
if a homeless guy fishing a grate hauls up

a dime or a nickel?—he's earned it!
I'm trolling this on November 19, 2008,
at 10 p.m. in one quick pass past
your lighthouse, & might not change it.

7.   (ROSE)

A SoHo party to say goodbye to *Prose*.
The issue which received me featured Paul Bowles,
Edward Dahlberg,Virgil Thomson.
I got a grand, big money, especially in 1971
before I left with wife & children for a year in Germany
as Fulbright lecturer to note-takers in Tübingen & Berlin
& Freibürg who wanted facts on Ahab & Prynne & Finn

& Whitman & Willy Loman. In any case, there I was
with Brockport pal Al Poulin in editor Coburn Britton's loft
while Richard Howard praised nine roses to his friend,
held up each number with a verse, nine
sips of champagne—all so elegant that I retreated
to boorhood, blocked my face when Gerard Malanga
tried to take my picture (I heard later that he'd appeared

in a Warhohl film). But a rose for me: Coburn's saying
mine was the only contribution not solicited,
that he'd been moved to tears when he'd imbibed it. . . .
When Al & I were leaving, we shared the elevator
with Richard who was helping & would signal a cab
for elderly Glenway Westcott, was kindly to him
in intuitive gay ways I've just begun to fathom.

8.   (Circuit)

My host SM tells me that famous JA blew him
        twice one party—

it was wild & bad sex in those days, he later wrote me.
        On the same poetry circuit,

I spent hours in front of his fire with WM, poet
        of quiet dignity who out of the blue said to me

readers didn't realize he was queer.
        No, I hadn't known, I conspired,

& this pleased him, did it, or confirmed for him
        the reticent poet he'd meant to be?

(I often taught his prophetic elegy "The Wreck of the Thresher"—
        austere, beautiful, "equal to our fears.")

Years later I met his young lover, RH, who cared for him
        in his post-stroke age

with executive devotion, I'd hear, & who said to me
        on their one Brockport visit

something still fermenting in me, that only barbarians
        drink wine chilled—

I laughed & now agree. But back to the circuit:
        that other RH walked behind my chair,

carressed my shoulders at a dinner party. (As I remember,
        I never did meet his partner,

SF, whose novel *Totem Pole* I reviewed for *Shenandoah*
        which never did print my praise.)

In any case, Frank, on that same trip SM & I had soup
        at the ouija poet's place—

he'd come to his Stonington door in tasselled velvety purple slippers.
    I got home with vertigo,

I admit, from all that fellow feeling, but this all passed—
    I was writing *The Swastika Poems*

for which SM would banish me, &, he wouldn't admit it,
    for being straight. (Years later,

in a cafeteria after his reading, Howl called out to me,
    "Bill, come on over & sit with us"—

this memory of inclusive AG has always inspired me.)
    But, yes, Christ, I was relieved

to oscillate home & just let those guys be:
    an All American college athlete,

I considered myself one of gay Walt's roughs but
    all you queers did scare me.

9.   (PORTRAITS)

Frank, I'm 68, Jimmy Schuyler's age
when he died—the bottom line was
he became a nut-case whose buttermilk-
encrusted glasses & demonic looks
split you & Joe from that threesome apartment.
Schuyler got to sleeping most of the day,
you kept awake at your MoMA desk,
Joe worked at the Holliday bookshop . . .
& every few days cleaned up the sperm-
addled glasses at "Squalid Manor."

In any case, you fellows/chaps/bitches was all—
Paul Goodman died at 60, & Edwin Denby
was a suicide—a bunch of crazies except
for the art that kept getting digested like a diet
of ambrosia, smelled like palmfuls of frogspawn,
revealed the Apple's soul; except for the art—
ballet of bedsheets on laundry lines
above the taxi horns, cats crying on canvas,
lofts of wire burnt & twisted into shape by torch,
a hexogram in a Cornell box. . . .

Here in my home village it looks like—
though I'll knock wood [he raps his desk]—
I'll make it to 69 & even beyond. Why not
visit? Don't you need some rest?
I've got three portraits of Saint Walt
on my western wall, one bought
at a flea market in New Hampshire.
"Give me O nature your primal sanities."
I don't know what he'd have made of Jimmy's.

Winter's here, water's drained from the Erie Canal.
I can angle down into its bed & across
the way you walked across Broadway
or plunged to West 47ᵗʰ, reflected in windows
filled with diamonds, to the Gotham where,

when I got there once or twice a year for years,
they couldn't keep your stuff in stock,
or so your partners liked to think
who checked your books for dedications
to see if they themselves were then immortal.
Angel, bundle with Walt across my portal.

10. (THE STRAND)

Larry Rivers jacketing a book of yours
that came with fifty others
from *Newsday* for review.
I didn't choose you: back then,
I couldn't—who could?—wing it with you.

In my old Vanguard Press days, I'd walk
from 424 Madison all those blocks
to the Strand. Frank, let's look into
that collection of drawings, *Self-Portraits*,
done for Burt Britton behind his privileged stacks

to see if . . . but, no, you tell me you
aren't there, I was mistaken. But
here are Jimmy Schuyler & Ashbery
& a hundred others you knew,
some intimately. . . .

I said to Burt I'd scribble a me only
if he'd not even glance at my ineptitude
until I left. I took about five seconds,
no more, but now I'm gladly there,
& here, however briefly, in Random House time.

What's the theory of art where you are?—
Cotter & I would like to know.
What self-portraits do you inhabit,
& does it ever snow? O'Hara's ghost
gestures to us through Broadway traffic.

11.   (ROETHKE)

At a museum in Michigan a couple weeks ago
       I bought a 2007 Pewabic paperweight,
a turtle, for a double sawbuck—the ceramic beauty's
            green glazes seem Spectacle Pond deep,

one pond of my Long Island childhood.
       You might have liked this object, Frank,
its head jutting precipitously into a corner.
           I should have gotten one for you, too.

In any case, I was in Saginaw for the Centennial
       of Theodore Roethke's birth, taught
a couple classes, lectured on 1/ his breakdowns
           that we shouldn't romanticize, &, 2/

his mysticism, a struggle of valiant spirit
       to escape from the slime. Years before, I'd slept
in his boyhood bed to which he retreated
           when his mind tendrilled dis-

sociatively dark on him. Outside his room,
       as you leave it, on your left, there's a wood rail
too low & weak to protect you from
           the abyss down the stairs, down

to his mother's quaking kitchen, down
       through Papa's orchid cellar, down
to where the ur-poet's heart
           throbs in green bedrock.

12.   (ART)

You sure hit it when you said
    "Dickinson's passion ignores
        her dazzling technique."
    But maybe her technique enables passion,
or maybe technique & passion are always

synchronous & fused, & not chosen,
    or maybe her technique is not dazzling
        but ellipsical variations on the ballad
    sutured into her thrice-broken heart,
or maybe into her brain, or both,

by way of her breath,
    or maybe passion never ignores technique
        but is oblivious until become hermetic,
    or maybe it's not technique, but craft,
as she served her austere father with gay prayer,

up & down the abyss of Amherst stairs.
    In any case, Frank, I think you'd agree
        that when Emily was spurned
    only the passion of art
kept her sanely crazy, crazily sane.

13.   (Meat / Flesh)

O'Hara,
meet Cotter,
by way of Craig's
Thanksgiving letter:

he writes me
after surgery,
#9
in 2009:

he wouldn't mind my
using him again:
in fact he
blesses me:

"so on my stomach for 70 minutes. I had no idea
how much tissue they were going to take out. I mostly
didn't feel anything during the operation, tho had one good jolt
of pain thru my entire body, I think from a cauterizing tool.
he apologized, etc., but lying there w/blood streaming down
my side, armpit, arm, I just didn't like it.

"I had in my mind 1/20th of what they took out.
I'm glad I didn't know in advance. then
I asked the doc to show me the chunk of flesh.
it was like 3 inches by 2 inches by ¾ inch deep.
u see all the layers of skin, then fat below. very
strange. I had no idea they could take that much out

"with a local anaesthetic. then took 20 minutes
of stitching. . . . (56 stitches, mostly internal ones.)
good thing about local is I could talk to doc during surgery.
so learned more about melanoma, and the kind I have.
will get stage later. it is too bad I have some
enlarged lymph nodes in that area too. if it's spread there—

"not good news. but will do some blood work in a week,
stitches out in 2 weeks, and oncologist soon
to look at all my recent tests. enough surgeries for one year.

but I should be glad I have insurance, and so far
have found treatment for my diseases. medical care is about
200K this year. w/out the job and insurance I'd be bankrupt.

"now wondering if I'll make it to 50.
my friend Anne says no need to consider that
for a couple of weeks. which is intellectually right
but not the way my mind is working now. it's more like—
do I try and get a trip to egypt in? do I move
from recluse to megarecluse and only read and write?

"and how do I keep making mortgage payments? etc.
mano has moved back in for bandage changing duties.
he's a good friend. I've read *Straight's Suite*
3 times now since you sent it. love it. be great
if you decide to find it a publisher. I took notes,
will write separate email when my mind is clear enough.

"SS (just realizing the abbreviation as I type it)
is very new. very broad range of styles w/in the poem,
which is exciting. interesting for me to see how u riff
w/material I have also riffed w/. isn't
leseuer's book magical? I'm so bummed
I never met him either. such a key person,

"as yr work shows. if I would have known
about FOH 10 years ago, I could've met joe.
joe apparently had 1 novel published, but I've never
been able to find it. SS is a brilliant piece,
and a great gift, especially that it came before
another operation. can't thank you enough for it.

"and can hopefully pay u back in verse some time.
I did write you another poem last week.
but the first draft strikes me as so horrible i
couldn't email it. my usual pattern is
to let things sit for 3-6 months after a first draft.
now that system is somewhat in question.

"on the bright side—if it's stage 1—I am now
cancer free. so try and get my mind around that,

w/ an abnormal brain MRI and chest CT—
well, the buddhists would suggest I shouldn't attempt
to trick myself. hope yr. all having a great Thanksgiving feast.
And hope yr. grandsons r getting some relief. best, craig"

What I keep re-
membering is meat,
meat & flesh, Lucian Freud &
painter Sig Abeles'
Self-Portrait with Horse Skull,
& a MAG exhibition
of tones of skin
gradations within which

our being beats
as within all beasts,
& now, Frank, Craig's
request to see

his excised "chunk of flesh,"
& you are typing while
sometimes in din & commotion
your art gets written

as Craig allays his fears
& aspires to be
a friend to poetry.
I posit this ain't

self-serving in me,
not a matter
of publishing praise
for my collage,

but for my reader
to imagine courage,
O'Hara's, Cotter's,
each & each for others.

14.   (THE MODERN)

that morning moment of reprise
when fluoride & coffee fuse

then the smell of both
seeming menthol cigarette breath

why conspire of paint the brain
apprehending how to mourn

just feeling extant & grounded
while in his coffin a dead beloved

whose every feature seems to see you
Rilke's archaic torso of Apollo

in any case when organs fail us
& feeling swells sculpted tear ducts

write winter orchids in the gift shop
whose red & mauve & ochre tongues drop

15.   (Winter Urine)

Frank, where the fuck were you
when I needed you

that freezing Sunday morning?
I was in your city, walking

the long way to the Strand,
when, uh-oh, I needed

to take a piss, & couldn't score
an open bar or diner or anywhere?—

I even asked a guy on his stoop
but he said nope.

I even offered him a fin—
he said shove it with a grin.

What kind of metropolis doesn't care
to relieve a tourist's instressed bladder?

I was so hard up I can't remember
if I got to the bookstore where

there existed a john I'd used before,
or if I pissed somewhere illegal,

maybe cursive in an alley
where I scribbled my own graffiti.

Why didn't you invite me?:
"Bill, make yourself at home,

"check out the Freilicher in the bathroom.". . .
But I forgive you who were already steam.

16. (Inquiry)

Not just the derivative, the futile,
but the revelatory ones, also.
They must be clogging up our landfills.
Where do all these paintings go?

There can't be walls for all of them,
or attics or closets in Malibu & the Hamptons,
or storage space in abandoned missile silos.
Where do all these paintings go,

offered by thousands, by tens of thousands,
by hundreds of thousands, in millions
by Jane & Jackson & Jasper & Willem,
but by others poetastering creation.

Sculptures, tapestries, assemblages,
light-wand constructs, ceramics, portfolios
aspiring to be immortal—what happens to it,
all that stuff from all those juried shows,

all those fairs & sidewalk exhibitions,
so much work from such prolific studios
where models yawn & stipple as they pose!—
where do all these so-called artworks go?

17.   (*"Simplicity! Simplicity! Simplicity!"*)

Cotter writes "u know I used to send Creeley
some drafts of cock-sucking and cum-eating
just to ask: how does a straight guy really
view this? He reminded me

"I had to do my own work, and write from where
I needed to write from—u know how beautifully
he phrased his emails and letters—
but he also admitted

"it could at first be a bit difficult to deal with,
but he was wonderful and accepting, and I get
that sense from your O'Hara suite." . . . Craig,
as sappy as this sounds, I just want

everybody to be happy except maybe
Leviticus who can go fuck a sheep.
It's not difficult for me to deal with, & shouldn't be—
I'm just not that interested,

& don't want you in my bedroom, either,
not even to imagine me with Han.
May all find the love I've found with her. Even
cretins should know it's in our genes.

18. (STILL, LIFE)

I try to be quiet mornings when Han still sleeps,
but my cereal bowl rattles,
or my banana is lodged beneath
oranges & apples in their graniteware bowl,

or cutlery dins when I remove a spoon. . . .

You'd admire her, Frank, the way she empowers others—
she's a breast-cancer survivor,
had a mastectomy years ago. She sleeps
inside me sometimes safely when she sleeps.

In any case, with my cursive I aspire

to semi-trance here, your composure even while
you pecked staccato on your Royal
when a poem was coming through you onto
canvas, now in stasis with you.

19.   (Eclipse: Dear Craig & Frank,)

years ago I wrote a strong & weak poem called "Suffering"
    about a hunter who equated his own arduous time in the woods
with that of the trophy buck he'd hit with a broadhead arrow
        & next day tracked & finished off with another.

"Suffering" appeared in a magazine called *Eclipse* & I'd pretty much
    forgotten about both until last evening when I found myself
standing in moonlight on a deer's back legs splayed out
        on the shoulder of a snow-banked country road

as my son-in-law knelt on the animal's spine because
    a third man, a stranger, was cutting its throat to put it
out of its misery after it was struck by someone else
        no doubt speeding when wilderness stepped out

or stood frozen in sudden lights veering around a curve.
    Under us, the deer snorted, the knife I'd rushed to the scene
was a dull kitchen utensil, I could hear the stranger sawing fur
        at the throat, working toward the spasming deer's jugular

to try to end its agony. I couldn't see enough to know
    if the victim was a doe or buck but it was strong,
its front legs snapping out as I kept my 200-pound balance
        as vehicles blasted by the four of us,

past our moonlit tableau I later couldn't erase from mind
    so suffered, yeah right, a semi-sleepless night,
begun like this: a spaghetti dinner at the farm,
        my son-in-law leaving with a plate of food

for a bedridden friend, then a call from him to come quick
    out to Route 31 where he & another driver had stopped
to drag a deer to the road's shoulder, & the deer was still alive,
        so they needed a knife, quick, & my daughter

took her largest from a drawer, my two young grandsons wide-eyed,
    & I drove off into February dark with the knife,
was there fast, & became with the two men & the deer
        a silhouette. I'll most remember the deer's snorts

& the sound of the less-than-ideal knife serrating fur
    with a low thrumming rasp, & black blood, until, at last,
wilderness lay still, I stepped off its ankles,
        the stranger who had done the awful

merciful work stood up & handed the knife
    to my son-in-law who wiped it on the deer's fur,
& then he & the stranger washed their hands in snow.
        The stranger called a friend of his to come for the doe—

maybe they could eat it if its meat hadn't been poisoned
    by one organ or another bursting at collision,
so at least there was this consolation of possible harvest,
        wouldn't we say? . . . Where are we except, again,

across an open field where the woods, at least in winter,
    cannot block moonlight, where the surviving deer
bed down lonelier this night than the night before?
        "As for me," as Robinson Jeffers says, I drove home

thinking of my beloved wife in unrelenting pain
    with fibromyalgia, who couldn't be with me,
or with our family that evening, & for a moment thought
        of drawing a razor across her throat.

20.　(COMPENSATION)

Truman & Tennessee,
　　　　& all you others at a party,
　　　　　　　the black guy Joe Ford, too—he
　　　　let himself get poached
(LeSeuer's metaphor) by a Lizst-like pianist.

In any case, dozens of gay artists there,
　　　　& Yukio Mishima
　　　　　　　who said he liked caucasian cocks
　　　　because they were bigger,
so after his half-year orgy here,

the Japanese supernova,
　　　　to reject his homosexuality,
　　　　　　　got married ruefully,
　　　　worked wildly at body-
sculpting to compensate for his

(LeSeuer's theory) small dick,
　　　　embraced emperor worship
　　　　　　　to tell the West to go ream itself,
　　　　& committed hara-
kira with a young soldier, his lover.

21.   (POSTSCRIPT)

The terror of the sublime—
        we're glad we weren't present.
                There are some experiences in life
        he was willing to forego, said lambent
meditative poet William Stafford

who praised places where the beautiful common happened,
        where no battles were fought, no monuments
                erected to evisceration,
        no novels written to stain
the bird- & star-pierced sky.

22.   (ARDOR)

I've not seen Pollock's *Lavender Mist*, not
in person & not by slide or print,
but Joe says it's "the visual equivalent
of a delicate perfume." You said that it

"fuses in a passionate exhalation."
In any case, we *are* that ardor when we
begin seeing unseen things. I've begun,
as snow whitens my downstairs windows,

to fuse your axe nose & reedy voice
as you compose indefinite sounds
that coalesce lavender scents
in our fragrance of works & days.

23.   (THE STRANGER)

July 31, 1959
    you looking over your poems since
Meditations in an Emergency

                some you think done
                      some just scraps of that
             & this just maybe compost

    you felt glum & dim
        "I don't glow at all"
    how did you trim

how light the wick again how
    get through being lonely
for your once ever incandescent self

34

24. (Fellow Feeling)

Today I bought a roll of the new gold-toned dollars,
this the 8th, Martin Van Buren, about whom
I know nothing except he looks empire. In any case,
I've had in mind to buy a roll & a few more each time
there's a new release—so far, so good—& in the future
get my four grandkids over to encase the coins.
I'll give each of them a couple sets to remember
such a day, if it ever comes to be.
I've got to live another decade while the U.S. Mint
stamps out this line of metal prexies.

This is what this has to do with you, Frank,
if you were wondering. I'm thinking ahead to when
my grandkids hit high school or college
& stop over for a visit on vacation break
to indulge their old forebear. I'm hoping for
a memorable occasion one of them might mention
when they're at my funeral to say sorry,
wiedersehen. In later years, they might tell their kids
of the day our family pressed coins into albums,
& their own lines would inherit this American story.

You gismed with dozens maybe hundreds of men
& then loved Joe & Vincent Warren & Bill Berkson
& all Walt's poets to come. For all I know,
maybe Martin Van Buren was gay—a golden
sheen crossed his face when I first
saw him today, he looked lonely, forlorn,
like maybe he had no idea that in 2008 anyone
would buy him in an Erie Canal village bank
for memory collections to send with grandkids into time.
O'Hara, I'm trying to find something here by writing

until I know what I can't intone
despite these being the first U.S. coins
with incised edges: *E Pluribus Unum.* If I'm
ever at your grave, I'll bury one beside your headstone
to assure you that you & Martin won't be forgotten even
if you never had grandchildren. Hundreds

declare you Poetry President of New York City in-
cluding Craig Cotter from Pasadena
who candles my desire to commune with O'Hara.
For him, now, this suite & a new dollar.

25.　(Tony Bennett)

I'm at the Walt Whitman Mall, it's almost Christmas, a couple
　　　　of you gay boys stroll by

who are in love, one's arm rounds his partner whose head rests
　　　　on the other's shoulder.

A high school chorus has finished singing, they're bunching back
　　　　through the Food Court

to where they'll catch their bus, a couple teachers are funnelling them,
　　　　& they're all in holiday spirits,

glad to be missing school, you remember those days, as I do,
　　　　those field trips, Frank & Craig,

& I'm glad for the students & teachers, & glad the partners are in love,
　　　　so golden glad that I think I'll

follow them to wherever they're going, maybe even watch them
　　　　as they make love so I'd get some

new sense of the asymmetrics, I'm only kidding, I'm some voyeur,
　　　　not, & the gay love-making

wouldn't thrill me as Walt might have thrilled as now
　　　　mall music swells O

down on your knees O hear the angel voices, & I do, as now they medley
　　　　into *Because of You.*

26.   (CHANGES OF ADMINISTRATION)

this village of mine ain't got the voltage of the Apple
        thronged jaywalkers or the stink of diesel
        or language ellipsis windows

a.m. I got up ate my usual cereal
        took a cup of coffee downstairs
sat in pajamas & old flannel bathrobe in my easy chair
        read a dozen of your I-did-this-I-did-that poems

liked thinking about you along your streets & at your desk
        dispensing MoMA info & shuffling papers
        & curating & dealing with some stuff
        & shuffling other stuff into a drawer again

wrote in my journal/diary I've been keeping 40 years
        24 closely-written blank books now buried in
        Rare Books & Special Collections at the U. of Rochester—
        they've made a copy for me so I still have me—
        & the next 19 volumes at the Beinecke at Yale—
        they still owe me a copy & I miss me but Nancy Kuhl
        who is Curator of Poetry is getting it to me—
        & I've already a few more filled blank books here at home
        a journal/diary posits an other who is necessary
        who is the Thou of Buber's I-Thou & thus witness
        as I posit you here, Frank

kept reading the Joe LeSeuer book & while I did I drafted
        3-4 sections of this *Straight's Suite* which by now
        you've heard as *sweet* too of course though you
        do something to me you didn't to Joe you
        sometimes scare me it's mainly the drinking
        though you don't mean to

got dressed just jeans over boxer shorts
        & a flannel shirt—Thoreau liked flannel shirts
        it took seasons for them to fit him he
        eschewed new clothes beware occasions that require
        new clothes not new wearers of clothes—

sure he was a scold & pain-in-the-ass old flannel-
head but let's keep fishing his pond for pickerel—

drove my gas gulper a mile fuck the environment
    & all future generations to the bank where I got
    the aforementioned Martin Van Burens
    but I've got five acres of trees I rationalize
    into balance for my depletions my spirit's
    a snail on Spectacle Pond's childhood lilystem

walked across the street to Rite Aide Pharmacy
    picked up a prescription
    for my wife's fibromyalgia & one my dentist
    issued me for some special fluoride toothpaste
    because my enamel deteriorates I wonder
    if Martin had wooden teeth like George Washington

my mouth is a minefield my dentist fills without novocaine
    I picture my toothless mother in her nursing home
    94 years old a force of nature there's
    a so-far-unpublished essay of mine I argue
    she's in sympathetic collusion with certain
    female sadist guards at Auschwitz & Belsen

stopped at the post office to mail a letter in which
    I decline to be U.S. Poet Laureate & another
    declining the Pulitzer Prize & another
    declining the National Book Award & another
    the Nobel Prize for Literature because I won't
    fly to Stockholm & have grown fond of my books
    that don't sell while those of "rising contemptuaries"—
    Frost's phrase—make it into the chains
    which are in any case phasing out poetry sections
    though I did see my *A Poetics of Hiroshima*
    which was a CLSC selection
    at a Barnes & Noble as though from another era
    as though they'd stocked it by mistake
    with other paraplegics among the electronics

drove another mile to my college locker room
    got changed & played basketball for an hour

with young guys & old guys though I'm the oldest
the young guys still don't mind playing with me
I perform a maneuver they admire
which they're not used to—the pass—
but my team lost 3-4 games for 11 baskets
because the other team had Roosevelt Bouie
who is 7' & starred at Syracuse & then in Italy
for about a dozen years & made real money
while I'm at it I'll team five end-rhymes cleverly
because Rosie respects me though instead of money
I wanted to use the word simoleons my dictionary says
only that simoleons is slang for dollars
I think dollars too are a kind of administration

took a shower got back into my gulper & drove another mile
to Subway picked up 3 foot-longs two turkey
& one tuna all on honey-oat but no cheese all three
with lettuce tomato onion don't forget the vitamin-C
green pepper Italian on the two turkey please O
I like the way Italy shows up here again
in Rome I kept visiting the Pantheon
but that's another story I'm sure you stood
there at Raphael's bier & genuflected as I did
even if you never got to Italy I know
Cotter wants to get to Italy maybe
the three of us will get to Italy & visit Dante

got home & made myself comfortable in front of the TV
& ate one turkey sub & a last brownie
from a Tupperware container from my daughter
I burped that container when I closed it again
as I burped her when she was a baby
watched the DOW fall again & Wall Street
scurrying around in a state of near panic bears
& bulls wondering what President Elect Obama
might think might be done about it one columnist says
all our problems stem from brilliant economists
I wonder what Martin Van Buren would do about it
how he'd preserve capital & capitalism or wouldn't bother
I like saying his name as you gather not once
in 40 years of voluminous writing has Martin Van Buren

appeared before this suite in any journal of mine
or poem or story but remember too as William Meredith said
poetry is the art of successful repetition & we know, too,
to repeat an image or even sounds like those five syllables
Martin Van Buren five coins of sound disrupt the linear
a poem dreams of being experienced all at once,
bam, like backfire or gunfire just as you step
from a curb to cross a street Frank I'd have liked
to cross a street with you to maybe
an exhibition or reading or better yet a party
except you got excised by a Fire Island dune buggy
you should have stayed in New York City
god ordains we die once with no repetition does she?

turned on my machine answered a few e-mails just
        to be amiable about stuff I'm not
        interested in but friends are I want to keep
        but you know how this sometimes does
        & sometimes does not assay because
        there's this ongoing unrolling of the life spool
        I get this image from Henri Bergson's
        Introduction to Metaphysics trans T.E. Hulme
        that I read in graduate school & had to go out
        into my garage to find just now to confirm
        what fun it is to unroll some such names
        T.E. Hulme like a blossom of Imagist time

went upstairs & took a nap I wish for this verse paragraph
        I'd had a dream to break up
        the pedestrian prosaic quotidien
        but I didn't so all I did was sleep
        for about a half hour & the millions of tiny rips
        that I understand we get in our bodies
        during strenuous exercise like basketball healed up
        I suppose all art is about rips in the artist ripping
        & healing or not healing because there's too much ripping

got back downstairs into this easy chair where
        I've been scratching this section out fast
        just in case I can hook something in the flow
        of traffic here I forgot to mention that I took

41

an apple downstairs with me too it's from
Kirby's Farm out on Ridge Road which was
a Seneca trail from Rochester to Niagara Falls
before we imposed these names on the keepers
of the Western Gate of the Iroquois longhouse
my apple was a red delicious we keep
a couple bushels in a wheelbarrow in our woodshed
cover them with blankets & eat fresh apples
all the interminable winter so what
if once in a while a crispin goes rotten
& I don't mean Wallace Stevens' comedian
Berryman said Stevens muttered so spiffy
rots into the real mush of a real rotten apple
& which Zennist was it well all of them who said
there are mountains inside every apple

in any case as I mentioned I got into this easy chair then
my wife got home from the mall & sat across from me
told me of some new bedding she got on sale
to replace bedding we've had for 25 years
& now she's gone upstairs & I've continued
writing this longest section of my *Suite* & this
ain't a hundredth of one day which may be
typical as it is & isn't while the prescient
books on my shelves are dumb without me
& blank books I've stocked are a trail for me
maybe you're somewhere waiting for me
if I ever tune my sensibility to your frequency
which ain't likely it would be too much
transformational voltage for me too much
informal bopping along with Broadway
which was *Breiter Weg* in my father's German
I'm stuck where I am maybe but you know
who knows when breakthrough will break through
when what enlightens me might not have enlightened you

my village is darkling now desultory snow
in the cone of a streetlamp outside my window
I could go play some poker this evening
I read you sometimes played cards but what kind
poker isn't gambling I'm pretty good at it

in the old days got to Vegas maybe twenty times
ten days at a time to learn discipline
but one of these I-did-this-&-I-did-that sections
is plenty enough a bad gamble for me Old Possum says
by way of J. Alfred that is not what you meant at all
I've got only about 30 pages of Joe's book to go
& in the end you'll die to cooperate with biography
which is one kind of trembling veracity
too bad you couldn't write a line like *I was walking*
at that moment your state of mind was
on the beach when I got hit & died

closed my notebook I swear I just now noticed its inside
    back cover JHANE BARNES for MoMA
    bought at MAG where my friend Grant Holcomb
    administers art's unchanging changes of administration
    I've got one other of these notebooks for other synchronicities
    opened my notebook again, wrote those last five lines
    though I was done with this section
    but how can we know conclusions
    as maybe I should have been I'm now
    going to close my MoMA notebook again
    snap it shut like a snapper's brain

I've opened it again I've snapped it closed again
    & so on until I-Thou & the ends of time
    like Niels Bohr I would also like to mention aluminum

27.   (DESERT)

In the end, in any case, we burn into form.
My old man smoked Camels, as yours did.
I'd sometimes steal a pack of palm & pyramid.
Inside, twenty pharohs waiting for flame.

28. (Toupee Song)

Trouble is that when old gay poets read young gay poets
they hear the queer notes
at the expense of other notes otherwise there.
Gray gay hair.

Trouble is that when young gay poets read old gay poets
they hear the queer notes
at the expense of other notes otherwise there.
Gay gray hair.

29.   (SONG)

In the old days
Italian tenors
before taking the stage
performed *fellatio*
on firemen in the wings—
this, they believed,

lubricated vocal chords
toward aria
when the soul O
deepest soul
both receives God
& beguiles the Devil.

30. (THE HAPPENING)

When you read at the Living Theatre & Kerouac
shouted up at you, "O'Hara, you're ruining American poetry,"
you flashed, "That's more than you could ever do,"
& exited the stage in a synapse of satori.

31. (PROJECTION)

Two grandsons laugh upstairs in the kitchen with Han.
Nick, seven,
is drawing & coloring in animals, one maybe

the Beanie Baby platypus she got him yesterday
at a garage sale
to add to his ark & farm & zoo & jungle imagination.

Jackson, eleven, is helping stack dishes,
sounds like. His wishes
for Christmas are a bass trombone & tropical fish.

Gays, unless you've got dough & manage
to adopt—well,
I suppose there are queer pleasures to assuage

what I'm projecting here as loneliness
without such children.
In any case, Frank, you genius poet lush,

don't be surprised if I sense empty spaces
(another Frost phrase)
in certain O'Hara poems enlivening gay works & days.

32.   (CLOSET HANGOVER *PILLOW TALK* SYNTAX)

Designer Calvin Klein introduced
even while himself pleasantly
his visitor explained tipsily,
"We just got into the City,
and heard about your party.
We hoped wouldn't you mind
if we just dropped

"in." Calvin said graciously,
"Of course not," &
the actor inside invited
where proceeded Rock
to get so plastered
that hardly he left
of his own volition

but had to be
caressed & cajoled
half-dragged,
half-carried
outside
down upside slo-mo
to his waiting limo.

33. (SURVIVORS)

Memory: playing the Platters' *Only You*
over & over for sometimes a half-hour.
I saw/heard them at the Brooklyn Fox—

"Only You," & "Twilight," & "The Great Pretender"—
when I was seventeen & Andy Caruso drove
four of us from Smithtown to city bedlam.

& I remember being heartbroken, for Karin,
though by now it shouldn't matter—
she's been a ghost for years. Lung cancer.

I saw her at our 40th high school reunion.
It's true that the heart doesn't keep time,
but mine didn't keep time for only her.

"Oh, Frank, if only you were here." Frank, hear
Joe LeSeuer's desire not just to be with you again,
but only with you & you alone.

34.   (New Lives)

The election's over, & there's Obama on the cover
of *Time* set up to look like FDR, tophat & cigar.
Have you seen it, Frank, from where you are
knocking down cranberry juice while you play guitar?
This guy's my first hero since maybe Mickey Mantle,
an entirely different character, more like you were
here on earth, at least for the drinking, forget baseball.
Ever run into him up there at your health bar?

The Mick owned New York for quite a while,
won the Triple Crown my junior year in high school—
that was 1956 when you & Joe moved downtown.
In any case, you cared squat about the Yankees,
but what's not to love about Casey Stengel
who once looked up & down his bench, forlorn,
& asked, "Can anybody here play this game?"
Please ask the Mick & Casey to send me their poetry.

35.   (THE CIRCULAR UNITS)

1.
   C. 1945 when my family lived in Queens
my sheepskin coat caught fire.
Smoke puffed out of my sleeves.
A man on the sidewalk
pulled my coat off & stomped on it.

2.
   C. 1950 in Nesconset my brother Werner
shot buttons off my sheepskin coat
with his BB gun. He told me
close my eyes, & I did.

3.
   Wenzel's sheep never did get a chance
to drop their big BB pellets
on cobblestones, which are orderly,
& Nesconset was not Italy.

4.
   John Brown drove his sheep
along the towpath of the Erie Canal
two blocks south of my Brockport home.
This was quite a while before
he saw the burning star.

5.
   Frank, James Dickey's "The Sheep Child"
speaks from a jar of legend & formaldehyde
in an Atlanta museum. That voice
is like smoke issuing from my sleeves.

6.
   My wild brother Werner tried
riding one of Wenzel's curled-
horn rams. He clutched hard before
he hit the ground.

7.
	Hereabouts we make fun
of a hick hamlet a dozen miles west
where the men are real men
& all their sheep are stressed.

8.
	In his kitchen, I watched Wenzel snip lambs' tails
with a paring knife against a cutting board, then swab the stumps
with iodine. Mrs. Wenzel made sugar cookies & gave us
a whole tin of them every Christmas. Frank, whatever transitions
there were were themselves in transit. I once stole bullets
from Wenzel, & once stole a solid lead pencil.

9.
	My favorite part of your "The Sentimental Units" is #7
wherein you say "There are certainly enough finks in the world
without going to a German restaurant." It's my favorite
for two reasons: 1/ Mickey Mantle was #7; 2/ I wish
all the finks would stop serving & eating veal—I hate those
little huts for calves that I see in finks' fields. I wish
every fink would have to spend a night in one of those huts.
& how inconvenient it is for me now—damn those finks—
that those huts are for calves & not lambs.

10.
	Given that I write quite a bit about sheep in my book-length poem
The Chestnut Rain which is about America's wars & America's farms
& farmers, & given Richard Wilbur's assertion that he's pretty sure
his poem is done when he's exhausted his present sense of subject,
I'm pretty much now done with this particular circular section
of my straight suite for you. But now, writing this paragraph
I've still found myself getting pissed off at the aforementioned finks.

11.
	Drove across Wyoming once when I did the Wyoming Poetry Circuit.
(I also drove across Wyoming when I did the Georgia Poetry Circuit.
I also drove across Georgia when I did the Connecticut Poetry Circuit.)
Out in that wild west there were historical markers about wars
between cattlemen & sheepmen. Those goddamn sissy sheep

were apparently not content just to eat grass but ate it so far down
that it didn't grow back, those goddamn sheep & sheepmen
who apparently wanted us all to live in barbed wire dustbowls.
The more I drove Wyoming, the more I hated them. In Cheyenne (notice
my surname buried in that word) I bought a cowboy hat, & if the Circuit
had been more lucrative, would have bought a rifle just in case
those goddamn sheepmen let their herds graze on my motel carpets
while I was trying to rustle some sleep. Truth is, I bought that hat
in Shoshone but wanted to embed my name in here like that,
& now will again: Cheyenne.

12.
    Once a dog kills a sheep you've got to shoot the dog or the dog
will keep killing sheep, is what Wenzel said. My dog Buster
wanted to kill cars. One hit him. He lay in our yard, dying.
My mother called Wenzel over to put Buster out of his misery.
Wenzel shot at Buster's head, shot his ear off. But his second shot
hit the middle of my dog's skull. I'm glad it didn't take seven bullets.
(I applied but was turned down for the Texas Poetry Circuit
which was probably administered by a bunch of finks,
& now, even if invited, I wouldn't want to be traveling across
Georgia & Connecticut & Wyoming while traveling across Texas.)

13.
    I love that image in Allen Ginsberg's "Wales Visitation"—
it's LSD, it's 1967, he's deranging his senses—"when sheep
speckle the mountainside, revolving their jaws with empty eyes,"
the receptive hypnagogic state, how poets graze & dream.

14.
    Who the fuck was Little Bo Peep, anyway, & why didn't she
keep her eyes open when her sheep wandered away?
Maybe they wandered all the way to Wyoming. Lots of men
got shot dead because of maybe Little Bo Peep's goddamn sheep.

15.
    Wenzel upended a sheep, tied all four legs together, sheared it.
The sheep *maaa'd* & bleated as he worked his electric shears.
When he was done fleecing it & untied it, it ran back to the flock
as happy as could be, it seemed to me, even with a few

54

red splotches on its back or sides where Wenzel sheared too closely.
Yes, how purely happy a shorn sheep was as it ran back to family.

16.
    Solid black painting, black sheep.

17.
    I have it in a closet—my Ph. D. diploma isn't even sheepskin.
Couldn't Ohio U. afford some fucking sheepskin? In 1967,
sheep everywhere were undergoing transformations,
undergoing transmogrifications, undergoing transluminations,
revolving their jaws in Wales for A.G.'s visions!

18.
    I forgive you, Little Bo Peep. I forgive everybody, even
the farmboy who coupled with that ewe who gave birth, after all,
to James Dickey's soulful poem, & I hereby forgive all finks.

36. (QUEEN)

Poet Craig Cotter from Pasadena wrote to say he'll be
       "knighting" me

"as an honorary gay." He makes this 70-year-old straight's day,
       the way he's befriended me,

& why shouldn't we all just mind our own fucking business,
       wishing all others well?—

so if Craig's letter says I'm not part of the problem,
       good for me,

I'll kneel as he taps me on both shoulders with his realm's
       pink sword.

37.   (A Flower)

Bastard angel Harold Norse walking with Tennessee Williams
        in their early days
crossing Sixth Avenue to Greenwich opposite the Women's
        House of Detention
hearing cries from above from the brick building & seeing
        at the top floor windows inmates
now calling down to them *Hey Sweetie youse*
        got a big one
wanna lay? Daaarling come on where ya goin?

& these make gestures & smooch the glass until one—this
        hits Harold & Tennessee hard—
breathes on a windowpane to fog it & then writes backward
        in large black letters
I LOVE YOU which phrase is like a flower em-
        anating from that grim
penal institution as the walkers as they'd meant to
        keep walking away from but into
the city that no matter what insists & lies I LOVE YOU.

38.   (Night Scene)

where is whose & what goes where
wine & booze glisten belly hair
sam's still configured in boots & chains
james's limp root complains
david's sphincter runs with blood
whose anus swelled & then contracted

meanwhile the sun cums on the river
gatsby's daisy toots her flivver
nick burns money from his trust
the eyes of doom stare down his lust
huck dreams of pleasing jim
their raft floats over catfish gism

what a night for these ten or twenty
penthouse elegance / moonshine shanty
marcus is waking in the pantry
cells are ringing for ned & harry
time to rise now rustle breakfast
caviar with prunes & toast

still on its easel yearns a painting
city arms a month past evening
splotches of yellow abstracted cabs?
what perry had in mind who cares
as long as edward can find his pants
before lyle arrives to rant

the painting knows whereof it sees
now a bandage for stephen's knees
laughter & memory conjoin
brandy hair-of-the-dog & aspirin
fellows pull themselves together
what need for meaning in this weather

his painting will be regifted soon
perry's impression of a cubist swoon
perhaps vaginal craters there

perhaps a curl of stefan's hair
viewers force futile associations
to color the rhythms of duration

night now alone in his straightened pad
perry approaches with trembling palette
his painting's receptive as a lover
what can he give him that lasts forever
he stands to deliver the coup de grässe
we leave him here, art's shangri la

39.   (DREAM TRACK)

friends & lovers & lovers of friends,
& friends' lovers' lovers, & friends'
lovers' lovers' friends, & friends
of lovers' friends' lovers whose friends

love friends' friends—a word
is a trance & a trance a word
& trains turn with their lighted beds,
friends in cars a roundhouse of friends

40.   (TRAIN)

(In Memoriam, Archibald Macleish, 1892-1982)

tonight writers I've known appear in the windows of a train
    crossing a trestle above a river

I am apart from them can look in on them cannot speak to them
    they do not know I am here

in each compartment a single candle—Archie immortal dreams of Paris
    cycles under plane trees with his friend Ernest

Jim Wright stares into Ohioan darkness prays thanks to Li Po
    for his new tongue

Ray Carver whispers a poem "Afghanistan" for his love who wears
    lapis lazuli on her finger

he doesn't know that John Gardner his teacher is so close I
    yearn to tell him . . .

but here is Anne in smoke laughing home from Bedlam in bright
    black hair & pearls

& Dick Hugo trembling back over Germany navigator
    in the stomach of a bomber

& now Red Warren seals a package that I've received *Brother
to Dragons* & a Stonehenge letter

& now John Berryman is aria in his whiskey again but here
    sings himself sober forever

& May Sarton in a rose suit sips champagne writes another year's
    intimate solitude

& brother Stafford in his morning sofa smiles at what is coming
    into the sound of impulsive being

& Etheridge Knight rocks in painsong in a prison cell on the porch
    of a Mississippi hut lord

what are they if I could touch them would my hands pass through them
    are their souls

in me in the last constructs of apparitional remembrance will I awaken
    within this train

before I see myself in the next compartment . . . the next . . . the next . . .
    for here is Archie again

standing at attention in his doughboy's uniform & now a glimpse
    of Hollis Summers my shy teacher

& Hellus & Al-Ubaidi & Poulin & Piccione & Brinnin & Carruth
    & Hoey & Creeley & Ignatow & Ai

& Hecht & Meredith & Booth & Logan poets who sang & still sing in me
    who will accompany me

as my train reaches here boxcars of books flashes of neural fire
    miscible candles in windows

that wash pale & blank over the hissed slowing
    of the wheels . . .

41. (Seventeen)

Craig, Frank, just once in my seventy years I stood within a revelation
    of falling petals.

I was seventeen, she'd left me months before, I could not believe
    I'd have to live without her.

Now, in April, somewhere beneath my breastbone,
    as Cummings phrased it,

a solitary bird sang terribly afar in the lost lands—
    I heard its plaintive notes,

& cruel spring had come again. I walked the margins of a farmer's
    furrowed field

where boulders brooded & woods began. A tangle of cherry trees—
    as though, I thought, to acknowledge

& assuage the emptiness in my chest—breathed for me & shook loose
    thousands of white petals. . . .

I'd like to testify that during those moments as the spiraling blossoms
    lit in my hair & fluttered

onto my face & arms I healed, became new again,
    glad in the world,

but nothing this clear came to pass that day, or would, or will,
    no matter how long I live

with my beloveds now—wife, children, grandchildren. But I remember
    the petal profusion & my acute

intuitions there within evidence of such oblivious beauty,
    such loveliness. . . .

I walked back to the road having experienced, I now know, a memory,
    this one, poignant enough at least

to make me wish I'd some day be able to let words cascade around you,
    touch you, my friends, from dead Karin. . . .

42. (THE NEW YORK SCHOOL)

I don't even know if you know this, Frank, but just
after you died Joe LeSeuer called Larry Rivers who said
"No! No! No! How can I live without him?"

They'd thought of flying you unconscious from Fire Island
to New York for a fifty-fifty chance you'd probably
not make it. You didn't. It wouldn't have mattered,

in any case, & no one was to blame. Off kilter,
your liver swelled & sulked. Willem showed up
with a blank check for the hospital. No use. . . .

At the impromptu wake at Joe's, Larry asked
for the cash in your wallet, would settle for that
so as not to have to dun your estate for the several

hundred smackers he'd lent you. Maybe I've flippity-
bopped this whole suite for you merely to embody
what Ned Rorem said: "I don't feel things deeply."

43.   (Peonies)

O'Hara, I sent your disciple Craig Cotter my book
    A Poetics of Hiroshima—

today his reply addresses how hard it is to write about
    certain subjects

like jesus—Craig's lower case—& dead grandmothers. He says my book
    made him remember

Grandmother Cotter hanging her geraniums in the garage on a clothes-
    line with wooden clothespins—

the flowers were cut down, he says, to stalks & a few roots to rest
    for the winter.

He says his Aunt Natalie still puts up her own delicious preserves
    made from grapes,

strawberries & raspberries his Uncle Clarence grows. He said
    he still gets

four jars for his birthday from her each year, & he spaces out
    eating the jam

so it will last him the whole year as it usually does except when he's
    with a partner like the last one who

went through the jars fast, & when Craig mentioned this to him
    his partner felt bad & maybe

this is part of why—though Craig doesn't say this—they broke up—
    & in this same letter

he mentions my "Blueberries Album" prose poem about photographs
    of Nazi perpetrators

partying at Auschwitz while gassings proceeded & tens of thousands
    of Hungarian Jews

were on their way in freightcars to this gruesome apex
of human time,

& Craig mentions peonies from his Michigan boyhood, big heads just
dripping with syrup,

ants crawling all over them probably sipping them until
kingdom come

& you know what I'm saying: that Craig's letter even while it isn't
about religion

& the horrifying slaughter of WWII, bodies & crematoria & bombs,
it sure is.

44. (3/12/11)

Frank & Craig, between acceptance of & proof of my *Straight's Suite*,
a few other sections arrived, & now this one in the hopeful state
of becoming, this morning, as news from Japan keeps assailing—
earthquake, tsunami, maybe another TMI/Chernobyl in the making,
who in christ can *process* it? I've just written in my journal—
how many journals & shrines & libraries & people are extinguished—
the end of Frost's "Once by the Pacific": "There would be more
than ocean-water broken / Before God's last *Put out the Light*
was spoken." I'm ravenous for some lightness of being despite
unspeakable death & turmoil, you know what I mean, not absence
of compassion, but surrender. The earth's

techtonic plates grind, upheave, we're all just a fucking inch
from oblivion, eternal life's a defensive fiction, so let's
celebrate with color, let's be companionable with candles,
let's write to invite survivors to MoMA not for insights,
not for so-called aesthetic appreciation of genius, not for
a tour of isms, but because, as Frost says, "It looked as if
a night of dark intent / Was coming, and not only a night,
an age." The wave that swallows Hollywood might be 100' high,
the fire that eats the Apple might sear Lady Liberty's gowned ass—
we'll resuscitate & bandage & mourn & rebuild & bury
as best we can, but let's, once more, for old time's sake, party.

45.   (SIMULATED)

Craig, just now in Harold Norse's autobiography
        I read of Frank O'Hara & John Ashbery
                dressed in bunny costumes, onstage
in a Kenneth Rexroth play, buggering one another.
        I picture puffy cardboard tulips in bloom,

the two young bunny-poets cavorting, free,
        in 1951, to the music of spring.
                I was eleven around that time, war
in the *Daily News* & *Mirror*, soldiers
        hearing Chinese bang blades on their helmets before

charging over American lines where we
        were decimated & retreated until
                massive reinforcements slowly won half
Korea back. The bunny-humping was simulated,
        maybe desperate. Flag-draped coffins. The dead.

46.   (A QUESTION OF COLOR)

The New York School of poetry seems
a giving-up

of fervor, of meaning toward closure,
for erasure

of blue, but by what & to whom for all
the right reasons?

47.   (LISTENING TO THE SUN)

I think when Craig is writing to me he's writing to you, Frank. I didn't
ask him about these things, but he knows I'm writing you, & knows
I know nothing about these things, so he writes me while sharing him-
self with you. E.g., Craig reveals

"the ex in that poem—mano—still lives w/me in the guest room
but is only here maybe one day per week, now mostly lives w/new bf.
i've been surprised he hasn't moved out—but he likes a private place
to retreat to, to retreat to our friendship,

"which has grown since we separated, so we're very close & i've had no
drama break-ups—i'm friends w/all my exs, men and women, or at least
the ones i can find—my two girlfriends from Michigan State,
rose and sarah—

"we're still in contact, see each other at least once per year.
same w/the bfs except alfred, but that was early development time
and i think his wife had him swear off even meeting me, not like
we were cheating on her

"w/sex, when I was 27, after our last meeting. but were we cheating
in what we talked about? if that is possible, w/a friendship too close
not for us but i guess for her. He even listened to christian fundamentalist
radio in his pick-up when he

"drove us around. i thought it was a joke, but i'm not sure, maybe his dry
sense of humor. on the other hand, he took us to one of our former
make-out spots, and on that trip to rochester asked me if I'd be up
to a 3-some w/ his wife

"so i was fine only wanting to be w/him but thinking the 3-some
could be interesting, but he apparently asked me first, not her . . .
and when she got the request, it did not go over well, as i suppose
u. can imagine. tho

"in the gay world open relationships happen between men after 3-6 years
almost universally, or as far as my experience takes me, which really
isn't even close to universal, is it?. . . well i can't thank u enough for
the wonderful section

"of yr long poem—it ended my work week the rite way,
getting my mind into art. and perfect for a rainy drive from pasadena
to the west side for a play and more art. . . . i woke up thinking
of lines for a new poem,

"and can remember what triggered it, but rarely write
in the morning, maybe will try to knock it out now, before
it's all gone. i'm so glad i've got some of my grandmother Cotter
in me. but here we don't cut down our geraniums, they blossom
all year. they're a different sub-specie

"than those in the east, and i wonder if they'd bloom stronger if
i cut them down each winter, but they just wouldn't freeze
in my garage and u can't put plants in these freezers
as they're electric and frost-free and suck out moisture.
have u ever tried

"to write a TALKING TO THE SUN POEM? i think it's
a great exercise, o'hara from mayakovsky. and no one knows
about that poem of frank's found in a kitchen (bathroom?)
drawer after his death when thankfully kenneth koch
rounded up all frank's poems

"in 2 suitcases o god this is getting too long but it's a dif-
ficult form cuz u have to have some superior—maybe god—
essentially telling u yr poetry is quite good. very self-
aggrandizing form, so very exciting and challenging.
I could never

"talk to the sun, but have one poem listening to the sun
that I think works and another talking to marlon brando
which i also think works. wish i hit that lotto so I could
travel whenever i wanted. do you ever see hepatica
in yr area? they could be

"breaking thru the snow soon. not february. but late march.
but so rare in my experience of walking michigan fields.
it's on my list to visit every part of the planet. thank u thank u
thank u. Craig"

48.   (PITCH)

Frank, Craig writes, "Bill"—
note how I move toward closure, line-
drive the three of us together—

"going to the batting cages turns out
to be highly predictive of muscle pain
(strong swings, autoimmune flares).

"got a new wood bat a couple days ago.
I'm sure I'll break it in w/in 18 pitches,
& hitting a hardball with a wood bat

"continues to be my favorite feeling in sports.
A nice hook-shot is good too but
hitting the hardball's the gold standard for me.

"so we build civilization w/our poems."
Craig, one game with two strokes on me,
I connected with my American ash bat,

drove the town-team fastball almost 400'.
I circled the bases & for fun slid home.
"so we build civilization w/our poems"

49.   (COHERENCE)

We had neighbor Nete over for supper last night Han's
sauerkraut & wurst & mixed vegetables
      then some Christmas cookies baked by neighbors
that Nete bought at a holiday sale at the Senior Center

         & why not flaunt margins

because I was reading Frank O'Hara's long late poem
to Bill Berkson it runs 16 pages of patter
      so then the three of us snow was drifting
         we went downstairs I'd built a fire

& we got cozy Han & Nete on the couch under comforters
& me in my easy chair we watched *The Book of Eli*
      in an early scene the pilgrim says something like
         If your hand touches me again
you'll lose it, so there the three of us were &

Iran with its nuclear weapons & Israel with its
      settlements in disputed territory
         & cholera in Haiti & whether or not
some steroidal pro would retire & my mother

      nuts & fierce & castigating in her nursing home said
         God would punish me & my family—well all
these things could go fuck themselves as they do in O'Hara
      who just keeps pushing the cuteness bar with his
         wine & food & which restaurant next to eat in
oh he's lonely & even desperate sometimes as NYC

glowers in its art grave such beautiful surfeit
      but the nail polish keeps polishing & mascara &
where is everybody anyway & foreign places show up
      & the North Star goes out & what's Richard Widmark
         doing here *Richard Widmark* on his own line
my friend Gavin met Richard Widmark who had the greatest sneer
      met him at Arthur Miller's place somewhere in Connecticut

& even the way I have it in me to come around now again
　　　　to Denzel Washington as he heads west on intuition
with his Braille bible the King James that he'll lose but won't lose
　　　　because he has it memorized no O'Hara
forswears coherence & closure they'll be the death of him
　　　　"is there anyone there" we'll keep our eye on the seismograph
at Fordham University as I kept my eye on one in Eureka
　　　　California when I headed out west but not
　　　　　　with King James rote in me anyway
Han & Nete & I sort of liked the way Denzel just
　　　　sliced up & arrowed & blasted all the bad guys
　　　　roll on great oceanic reels of cinema roll on

& I kept placing split ash & maple in the fire pre-apocalypse
　　　　here in my home for now I heard today I'll have five poems
　　　　　　in *Poetry International* let's have a bloody mary
on Mauna Loa while we reminisce about a personal letter
　　　　once received from Isak Dinesen
　　　　　　I got a holograph card once no kidding from Yoko Ono
because I'd sent her my poem for Lennon called "The Colony"
　　　　in which ants crawl through the building in Manhattan
　　　　　　where she & her husband lived & there's a lot
of red in my poem reddishness & glow as I remember
　　　　I'm lonely with O'Hara for that glow he sometimes felt

so let's have another biscuit on Yom Kippur
　　　　but the future always falls through the past & vice versa
& there's a loss of blue & red for that matter
　　　　in so many abstractions these days but so what what
　　　　　　matters is to keep rolling as the ocean does

remember the time we never hid behind dunes on Fire Island
& O'Hara doesn't think much of Wally Stevens who did
　　　　keep rolling on in the most beguiling ways
what can relieve our sexual boredom Eli is chaste
as he marauds his way westward with the whole gospel in his heart

　　　　Emerson asked what is a farm but a mute gospel but
I met Tom Holmes at Java Junction yesterday for redundant java
　　　　we spoke of Vorticists again I call him Vort
　　　　but Frank I'm sorry to be letting you down but I just

can't help myself it's in my genes
to mention Richard Widmark again that tough guy
        no one dared call him faggot let's stare into & smell
any gangrene in the poem's inner ear
never seek to know all the secrets of West 47th it's
        impossible man all those diamonds will glitz your eyes

& all the books at the defunct Gotham forget it I
        could keep rolling on like celluloid or the ocean some-
one said the most important thing that ever happened
                in the history of all American poetry was that Saint
Walter stood at the shore & watched the waves
        maybe so but you could argue too it was King Jimmy
that Melville memorized & Walt had in his American sinews
        & there were other sparks arriving from far galaxies
I need space here windy drifting spaces to honor O'Hara
        who'd have liked to sip champagne from the crystal glasses
I saw at VOA yesterday what was their story how
        did they get there I can't help myself Frank as

Denzel arrives at is it Alcatraz fortified by the purified survivors
                who believe in memory & want to start over he
        begins to recite they robe him in white they shave his beard
& head they take down verse & chapter & every book written /
        translated by King James's men who the fuck were they anyway
we hear Jesus looked over their shoulders
        with the Holy Ghost glowing in his heart so let's you & I
this snow-blowing day arise & go for a long walk along

                        the Erie Canal towpath I'm only kidding
let's sit & talk at a table alongside the Park Plaza Hotel's
        dark bar do they have candles there
                while the story of your helpless city composes itself not
in coherent seriousness but scattered collages
        of almost-song. . . . I can hear the shofar but
                here comes the el
with this 102nd line just for the el of it I counted

        I once shared a cab with John Wieners
told him I loved his "Poem for Trapped Things" I saw
        John & Charles Olson at Cortland kiss long & long

a wet tonguekiss after Olson's non-reading that was all
    silences & grunts

       Frank did you feel trapped at Harvard with John Ciardi
    I don't feel as trapped now that my mother's dead
Ciardi once wrote me that death was everything & nothing

I've now seen Pollock's *Lavender Mist*, online,
    but have seen my cover Freilicher in person,
       up close, walked through its voyeuristic window
  without upsetting its plant in its pot in its blue & white bowl
on its transparent glass or plastic table inside the painting's

clear lavender-puce Long Island sky under which probably
    everybody is wealthy except for me
but there are great white sharks prowling the waters out there
    & what kind of plant is that, anyway,

Eli would have protected Allen Ginsberg despite Leviticus
    Allen's skin was a holy robe
    farmkids are playing baseball in a meadow in Wisconsin

    the number 52 is always an homage to Walt Whitman

& these last two dozen lines for Nete & Denzel & all
    I've mentioned here
        because I couldn't help myself

50.   (Email from Cotter on O'Hara's Birthday)

"could've

"burned down my condo yesterday.
Have 4 throw pillows on my couch.
I tend to throw them around.
So had tossed one, was eating breakfast
and watching TV news. Smelled something
that I thought was someone cooking.
Then noticed one pillow was leaning

"against the floor heater—
I have a little model that rotates.
So it was smoking
& by the time I got to it it
had just caught fire. Got it
into the sink. But
if I had gone to take a shower it

"would've"

51.   (THE ROSES, 2011)

A rose for the Egyptians
  A dozen roses for the Egyptians
    A hundred roses for the Egyptians
      A thousand roses for the Egyptians
        A million roses for the Egyptians
          Six million yellow roses for the Egyptians

52. (Country Mouse)

If a poem is not about thought but *is* thought,
then I won't think to say how reading you, Frank,
sometimes feels as though your thought reads me,

as, even now, rain may well be pelting asphalt
on West 47th where the Gotham used to be,
where I bought poetry so hopefully

so many times. In any case, I think maybe
your city *is* your dictionary but not of de-
notations but of syllables, of sounds,

but a million times as thick as the *OED*,
but I don't want to need a magnifying glass
to feel thought's coalescing wetness,

or do I?—yours is the cloud of thought raining
until the self becomes a hum which now forms
your gay body, the poet's melody, thought's song.

A NOTE ON THE AUTHOR

William Heyen lives in Brockport, New York. A former Senior Fulbright Lecturer in American literature in Germany, he has won prizes and awards from the NEA, the John Simon Guggenheim Foundation, and the American Academy & Institute of Arts & Letters. His poetry has appeared in *The Atlantic*, *The New Yorker*, *Harper's*, *The Southern Review*, *American Poetry Review*, and in hundreds of other periodicals and anthologies. His *Crazy Horse in Stillness* won the Small Press Book Award in 1997, *Shoah Train: Poems* was a Finalist for the National Book Award in 2004, and *A Poetics of Hiroshima* was a Chautauqua Literary & Scientific Circle selection for 2010. A list of his books appears in the front of this volume.

OTHER RECENT TITLES FROM MAYAPPLE PRESS:

Lydia Rosner, *The Russian Writer's Daughter*, 2012
    Paper, 104pp, $15.95 plus s&h
    ISBN 978-1-936419-10-4
John Palen, *Small Economies*, 2012
    Paper, 58pp, $13.95 plus s&h
    ISBN 978-1-936419-09-8
Susan Azar Porterfield, *Kibbe*, 2012
    Paper, 62pp, $14.95 plus s&h
    ISBN 978-1-936419-08-1
Susan Kolodny, *After the Firestorm*, 2011
    Paper, 62pp, $14.95 plus s&h
    ISBN 978-1-936419-07-4
Eleanor Lerman, *Janet Planet*, 2011
    Paper, 210pp, $16.95 plus s&h
    ISBN 978-1-936419-06-7
George Dila, *Nothing More to Tell*, 2011
    Paper, 100pp, $15.95 plus s&h
    ISBN 978-1-936419-05-0
Sophia Rivkin, *Naked Woman Listening at the Keyhole*, 2011
    Paper, 44pp, $13.95 plus s&h
    ISBN 978-1-936419-04-3
Stacie Leatherman, *Stranger Air*, 2011
    Paper, 80pp, $14.95 plus s&h
    ISBN 978-1-936419-03-6
Mary Winegarden, *The Translator's Sister*, 2011
    Paper, 86pp, $14.95 plus s&h
    ISBN 978-1-936419-02-9
Howard Schwartz, *Breathing in the Dark*, 2011
    Paper, 96pp, $15.95 (hardcover $24.95) plus s&h
    ISBN 978-1-936419-00-5 (hc 978-1-936419-01-2)
Paul Dickey, *They Say This Is How Death Came into the World*, 2011
    Paper, 78 pp, $14.95 plus s&h
    ISBN 978-0932412-997
Sally Rosen Kindred, *No Eden*, 2011
    Paper, 70 pp, $14.95 plus s&h
    ISBN 978-0932412-980

For a complete catalog of Mayapple Press publications, please visit our
website at *www.mayapplepress.com*. Books can be ordered direct from our web-
site with secure on-line payment using PayPal, or by mail (check or money
order). Or order through your local bookseller.